_____

Presented To:

_____

Presented By:

_____

Date:

How great is the love the Father has lavished on us,
that we should be called children of God!
And that is what we are!

1 John 3:1 NIV

We need *good* fathers in our homes

whose hearts are full of *grace*,

Who by their *love* and earnest prayers,

make home a pleasant place.

Walter Isenhour

A FATHER'S WORDS OF WISDOM

A Collection of Fatherly Wisdom and Inspiration

BLUE SKY INK

Brentwood, Tennessee

SUCCESS

Success seems to be largely a matter of hanging on

after others have let go.

William Feather

Be strong and do not
give up, for your work
will be rewarded.

2 Chronicles 15:7 NIV

WISDOM

Wisdom is a good thing.

It's like getting a share of the family wealth.

It benefits those who live on this earth.

Ecclesiastes 7:11 NIrV

The *best* way out is *always* through.

Robert Frost

Suffering produces perseverance;
perseverance, character;
and character, hope.

Romans 5:3–4 NIV

If any of you lacks wisdom,
he should ask God, who gives
generously to all without finding
fault, and it will be given to him.

James 1:5 NIV

Every *father* is to be the instructor and living example for his *children* in obeying the commands of God and the teachings of Jesus.

Catherine Marshall

FATHER

I watched a small *man* with thick calluses on both hands work fifteen and sixteen hours a day. I saw him once literally bleed from the bottoms of his feet, a *man* who came here uneducated, alone, unable to speak the language, who *taught* me all I needed to know about *faith* and *hard work* by the simple eloquence of his example.

Mario Cuomo

Time, not money, is the

Real life is not measured by how much we own.

Luke 12:15 NLT

real currency of our lives.
R. Triplett

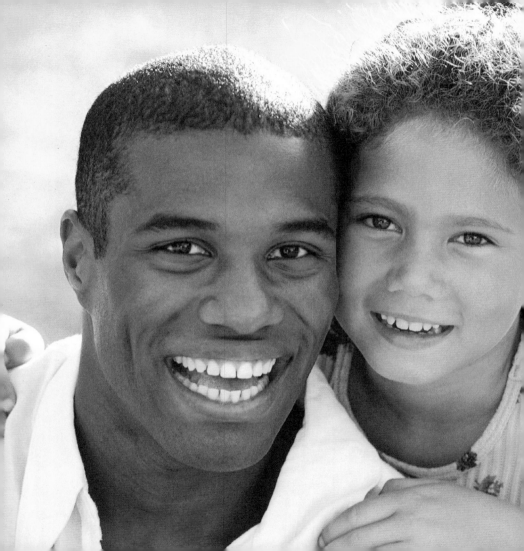

Let your ears listen

to wisdom. Apply your

heart to understanding. Call

out for the ability to be wise.

Cry out for understanding.

Proverbs 2:2–3 NIrV

There are no impossible

dreams—just our

limited perception of

what is possible.

Beth Mende Conny

With God all things are possible.

Mark 10:27 NKJV

WISE

Become wise, dear child, and
make me happy; then nothing
the world throws my way
will upset me.

Proverbs 27:11 THE MESSAGE

There is something ultimate in a

father's love, something that

cannot fail, something to be

believed against the

whole world.

Frederick W. Faber

Everyone you meet

knows *something*

you don't know.

Be willing to *learn*

from them.

A wise man will hear and increase learning.

Proverbs 1:5 NKJV

A careful man I ought to be;

     a little fellow follows me.

I do not dare to go astray,

     for fear he'll go the self-same way.

I cannot once escape his eyes;

     whatever he sees me do he tries.

Like me, he says, he's going to be,

     that little chap who follows me.

I must remember as I go,

     through summer's sun and winter's snow,

I'm building for the years to be,

     'cause a little fellow follows me.

like daddy

Laughter adds richness,

texture, and color to

otherwise ordinary days.

Tim Hansel

laughter

A happy heart makes the face cheerful,
but heartache crushes the spirit.

Proverbs 15:13 NIV

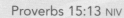

Wisdom is a tree of life to those who embrace her;

happy are those who hold her tightly.   Proverbs 3:18 NLT

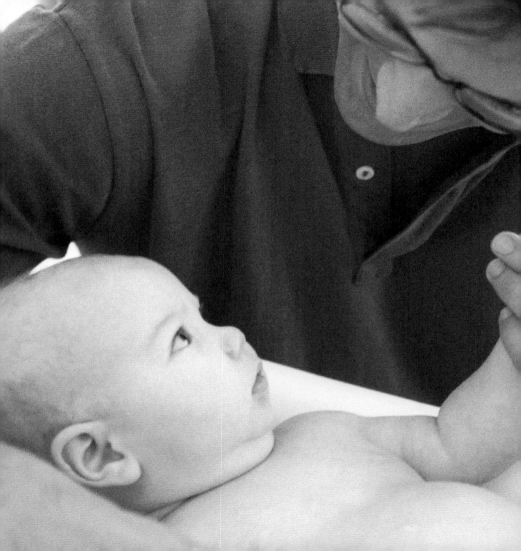

Whatever you do, do all to the glory of God.

1 Corinthians 10:31 NKJV

A great deal of *good* can be done

in the world if one is not too careful

who gets the credit.

George Herbert

Watch your step.

Use your head.

Ephesians 5:15 THE MESSAGE

My *father* didn't do anything unusual. He only did wha

daddy

dads are supposed to do—*be there*.   Max Lucado

Life is a coin. You can spend it any way you wish, but you can *only* spend it once.

Lillian Dickson

What is your life?
It is even a vapor that
appears for a little
time and then
vanishes away.

James 4:14 NKJV

God took the *strength* of a mountain,

the majesty of a tree,

The warmth of a summer sun, the calm of a quiet sea,

The generous soul of nature, the comforting arm of night,

The *wisdom* of the ages, the power of the eagle's flight,

The joy of a morning in spring, the *faith* of a mustard seed,

The *patience* of eternity, the depth of a family need,

Then God combined these qualities;

when there was nothing more to add,

He knew His masterpiece was complete,

And so, He called him . . . *Dad*.

Unless you are faithful in small matters,
you won't be faithful in large ones.

Luke 16:10 NLT

Faithfulness in little things

is a *big* thing.

Saint John Chrysostom

I pray for you constantly,

asking God, the glorious Father

of our Lord Jesus Christ, to give

you spiritual wisdom and

understanding, so that you

might grow in your

knowledge of God.

Ephesians 1:16–17 NLT

My *obligation* is to do the right thing.

The rest is in *God's* hands.

Saint Francis de Sales

If you know that [God] is righteous, you know
that everyone who does what is right
has been born of him.

1 John 2:29 NIV

Real wisdom, God's wisdom, begins with a holy life and is characterized by getting along with others. It is gentle and reasonable, overflowing with mercy and blessings.

James 3:17 THE MESSAGE

My *father* would pick me up and hold me
high in the air. He dominated *my life* as long
as he lived, and was the *love* of my life
for many years after he died.

Eleanor Roosevelt

If you *find* find God, you find *life*;

if you miss *God*, you miss

the whole point of living.

Kenneth Pillar

Draw nigh to God,
and He will draw nigh to you.

James 4:8 NKJV

Be kind to thy father,

for when thou wert young,

who *loved* thee so fondly as he?

He caught the first accents that

fell from thy tongue,

and joined in thy *innocent* glee.

Father's Words of Wisdom
ISBN 1-59475-027-0

Copyright © 2004 by GRQ Inc.
Brentwood, Tennessee 37027

Published by Blue Sky Ink, a division of GRQ Inc.
Brentwood, Tennessee 37027

Editor: Lila Empson
Compiler: Snapdragon Editorial Group, Inc., Tulsa, Oklahoma
Design: Diane Whisner, Tulsa, Oklahoma

Printed in China.